the
wonder®
BREAD
COOKBOOK

the wonder® BREAD COOKBOOK

an inventive and unexpected recipe collection

from Wonder®

FOOD PHOTOGRAPHY BY Leo Gong

TEN SPEED PRESS
Berkeley | Toronto

Ten Speed Press
Box 7123
Berkeley, California 94707
www.tenspeed.com

Distributed in Australia by Simon and Schuster Australia, in Canada by Ten Speed Press Canada, in New Zealand by Southern Publishers Group, in South Africa by Real Books, and in the United Kingdom and Europe by Publishers Group UK.

Cover and text design by Betsy Stromberg
Food styling by Karen Shinto
Prop styling by Natalie Hoelen
Food styling assistance by Jeffrey Larsen
Photography assistance by Harumi Shimizu

Library of Congress Cataloging-in-Publication Data

The Wonder Bread cookbook : an inventive and unexpected recipe collection from Wonder / food photography by Leo Gong.
   p. cm.
  Summary: "The official Wonder Bread historical reference and cookbook, with sweet and savory recipes from fans showcasing the many ingenious ways to cook with Wonder Bread"—Provided by publisher.
  Includes index.
  ISBN-13: 978-1-58008-807-7
  ISBN-10: 1-58008-807-4
  1. Cookery (Bread)
  TX769.W733 2007
  641.8'15—dc22

                         2006034395

Printed in China

1 2 3 4 5 6 7 8 9 10 — 11 10 09 08 07

Contents

ACKNOWLEDGMENTS • ix

PREFACE • xi

A WONDERFUL LIFE: HISTORY OF AN ICONIC
AMERICAN BREAD • 1

CHAPTER ONE • • • • • • • •
Good Morning Wonder Bread
• • • • • • • • • • • • • •

Wonder Bread Eggs • 14

Wonderful Bird's Nest • 15

Pigs in a Wonder Blanket • 17

Baked Wonder Omelet • 18

Apple Wonder Waffles • 19

Cinnamon Wonder Waffles • 22

Wonder Eggs Royale • 23

Wonder Crullers • 25

CHAPTER TWO • • • • • • • •
Wonder Bites
• • • • • • • • • • • • • •

Wonder Blintzes • 28

Wonder Cream Cheese Bites • 30

Three Wonderful Pieces • 31

Wonder Parmesan Bread • 33

Wonder Bread Pepper Snack • 34

Wonder Bread Balls • 35

Wonder Asparagus Rolls to Die For • 36

Old-Fashioned Cinnamon
Wonder Toast • 39

Wonder Beef Cups • 41

CHAPTER THREE • • • • • • • •

Wonder Sandwiches

• • • • • • • • • • • • • •

Grilled Peanut Butter, Jelly,
and Wonder • 44

Wonder Chip "Wich" • 46

Grilled Baloney and Wonder • 47

Wonder Omelet Sandwiches • 49

Wonder Sausage and Peppers • 50

Wonder Trail Mix Sandwich • 51

Wonder Kid Sandwiches • 52

CHAPTER FIVE • • • • • • • •

Sweet and Fruity Wonder

• • • • • • • • • • • • • •

The Most Wonderful
Apple Pie Squares • 64

Wonder Pear Cobbler • 66

All-American Peach Pie Wonder • 67

Wonderstrudel • 69

Wonderful Napoleon • 71

Wonder Easter Egg Sandwich • 74

CHAPTER FOUR • • • • • • •

Baked Wonder

• • • • • • • • • • • • • •

A Perfectly Wonderful Casserole • 57

Sweetened Tomato and
Wonder Casserole • 58

Wonderfully Crunchy Chicken
Casserole • 59

Tropical Wonder Casserole • 60

CHAPTER SIX • • • • • • •

Wonder Bread Pudding
and Crêpes

• • • • • • • • • • • • • •

Top-of-the-Morning Wonder
Bread Pudding • 78

Wonderful Crêpes Suzette • 79

Wonder Caramel Apple Bread
Pudding • 82

Grandma's Wonder Bread Pudding with
Lemon Sauce • 83

Wonder Apricot Pudding • 85

CHAPTER SEVEN • • • • • • • •

It's a Wonder

• • • • • • • • • • • • • • •

Pilgrim Pies • 88

De Luxe Bridge Loaf • 89

Swedish Pork Chops • 90

Jellied Eggs • 92

Creamed Fish in Wonder Patty Shells • 93

Mrs. Proctor's Devilled Crab • 94

Delicious Lenten Pudding • 95

INDEX • 96

Acknowledgments

Interstate Bakeries Corporation (IBC), the baker of Wonder bread, would like to thank the following individuals and organizations for making this special recipe collection possible:

IBC's Rich Seban, Stan Osman, and Theresa Cogswell, who every day devote their considerable talents to continuing to advance the Wonder brand;

Alvarez & Marsal for bringing keen business insights to IBC and supporting one of America's greatest brands;

Hannah Arnold, who conceived this book and wrote the introduction chronicling the history of Wonder bread, and the team at Linden Alschuler & Kaplan, Inc., Public Relations;

Kathy Moore and Roxanne Wyss of Electrified Cooks for skillfully testing—and tasting—these exciting recipes;

and the millions of Wonder bread fans, who have made it one of the most popular brands in history.

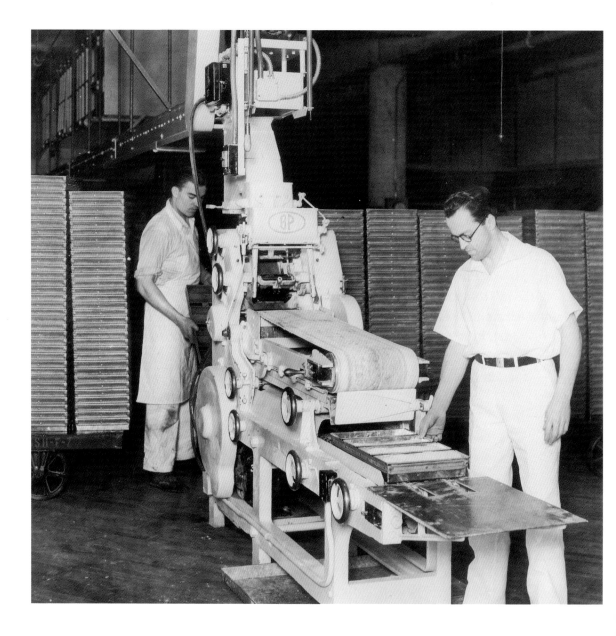

Preface

For more than eighty-five years, Wonder bread has been an American staple—a product that has soared to iconic status, helping to build more than a few "strong bodies" along the way.

We want to thank all of the Wonder enthusiasts who made this special book possible. From soufflés and sandwiches to blintzes and bread balls, this inventive and unusual collection features the best-of-the-best savory and sweet Wonder bread creations from America's kitchens and the Wonder archives.

—Interstate Bakeries Corporation, baker of Wonder bread

A Wonderful Life: History of an Iconic American Bread

IF BREAD IS THE STAFF OF LIFE, AMERICA HAS RUN ON WONDER.
Go ahead and admit it: you love the stuff. Even after all these years, you find nothing beats mushable, squishable, toastable, simply unforgettable Wonder bread. Don't worry; you've got plenty of company. Any way you slice it, Wonder is the best-selling brand of white bread in the country—to the tune of more than 127 million loaves a year. That stacks up to about 1.3 billion sandwiches, in case you were, well, wondering.

So what accounts for this enduring appeal? What more can be said about the product that inspired the phrase "the best thing since sliced bread"? How do you capture the essence of a brand that was promoted by a famous quartet of singing bakers, pitched by Howdy Doody and Buffalo Bob, helped to build strong bodies, and coined the phrase the "Wonder Years"? It comes down to this: America just wouldn't be the same without Wonder bread.

And Wonder bread wouldn't be Wonder bread without Elmer Cline.

The year was 1921. The world was changing in exciting ways, and in the heartland of the home front the Taggart Baking Company was gearing up to introduce a new, large 1½-pound loaf of bread.

As vice president for merchandising development at Taggart, whose label was once described by the *Indianapolis Star* as the "perfection stamp of bakery goods," Cline was in charge of branding—naming the product and developing the packaging. While taking in the International Balloon Race at the Indianapolis Speedway, Cline was captivated by the scene of hundreds of balloons creating a kaleidoscope of color as they floated across the Midwestern sky. Inspiration struck when he was filled with wonder and, as the story goes, a brand was born.

WONDER
"Marvel"
—N. W.

WONDER?
How often do you use this word every day?
—check yourself

WONDER
what?

WONDER
noah Webster says:
—Something exhibiting great skill, or other remarkable quality.
—Marvel.
—Something out of the ordinary.

WONDER
You've wondered now for several days,
You've checked yourself in many ways.
This word, you know, you'll not forget
But the real WONDER is unknown yet.
Just remember this—you'll never find
A WONDER of a better kind.

When it came to conceiving the bread's launch, Taggart decided to make consumers wonder a bit, too. Weeks in advance of the actual debut, the company ran a series of blind ads to pique interest and curiosity about the new product.

The answer to the mystery was officially revealed in an ad published on Saturday, May 21, 1921, in the *Indianapolis News* and again, two days later, in the *Indianapolis Star*. It read:

WONDER

So now the mystery we will end,
And to every home a message send,

A message that brings joy to you,
To mother, father and grandma, too,

To Mary, Betty, Jack and Joe,
For all the family will learn to know,

The meaning of this wonder word
That every one has read and heard.

A new delight with every bite,
Both morning, noon and every night,

For Mary Knows, you know her well,
And many a truth she's had to tell,

But now the best she ever knew,
She gives in this new loaf to you,

For as Taggart leads, they're still ahead,
And now it's

Taggart's WONDER BREAD

The Bigger, Better Taggart Loaf
You Will Know It by the Wonder Wrapper

P. S.—Place your order for WONDER BREAD, the new Taggart wrapped loaf, with your grocer Monday. He will have it beginning Tuesday, May 24

Yo-Ho! Yo-Ho! Yo-Ho!
We are the bakers who mix the dough
And make the bread in an oven slow
And work for the Continental
We are the bakers in spotless white
Whose pans are polished and shining bright
Who bake the bread that is always right
Hurrah for the Wonder bakers
Yo-Ho! Yo-Ho! Yo-Ho!

It didn't take long for Wonder bread to take off. When Taggart was acquired by Continental Baking Company in 1925, the company began marketing the brand nationally.

A singing quartet known as the Happy Wonder Bakers was hired to promote Wonder on national radio. Performing in poofed toque hats and white uniforms, the jolly bakers popularized the theme song, "Hurrah for the Wonder Bakers," belting out jingle-like lyrics that began: "Yo-Ho! Yo-Ho! Yo-Ho! We are the bakers who mix the dough and make the bread in an oven slow." Talk about singing for supper.

And just in case consumers couldn't find enough uses for Wonder, the company brought America Alice Adams Proctor, who was to bread what Betty Crocker was to cake—a lifelike but fictional expert who was featured in pamphlets giving busy homemakers meal-planning tips and a variety of recipes using Wonder bread. Proctor may have been a figment of marketers' imaginations, but the homespun personality radiating from booklets with matter-of-fact titles such as "Breakfast Menus" and "New Suggestions for Lenten Dishes" offered "flashes of inspiration to charm the flagging appetite and ease the family budget" and struck a chord with consumers, who were invited to write to Proctor. She became a fixture in Wonder bread promotions for decades.

Then, in 1930 came the slice that made history. Wonder became the first major brand to distribute sliced bread—a significant milestone for the industry and for American consumers. Considering the ubiquitous phrase, "the best thing since sliced bread," it goes without saying the move was a hit. But initially, consumers surprisingly needed some reassurance. To convince skeptics that "Wonder-Cut" bread wouldn't dry out, the company offered free sample slices wrapped in wax paper and distributed fliers to grocers with the message "Feel It and Find Out." The slices quickly caught on and became standard fare until a World War II steel shortage led to an industry-wide slicing suspension in 1943. "Lady! Sharpen Your Bread Knife," read an ad, following the government's directive. Thankfully, slicers were back in business less than two years later.

Wonder was not only a name, but it was also a theme for marketing the product, as the company came up with a continual stream of promotions designed to create a sense of wonder. In addition to clever advertisements, there was the Wonder Ship, a blimp emblazoned with the Wonder bread logo and trademark bright colored dots that appeared at various municipal airports. Then there were the World's Fairs in Chicago and New York in 1934 and 1939, where full-scale working bakeries were set up at the fairgrounds, complete with ovens and other equipment used at the time to bake Wonder bread.

For the Chicago fair, which celebrated the theme of technological innovation, the company issued a special edition of *The Wonder Book of Good Meals*, in which Alice Adams Proctor offered more than twenty pages of ideas, "cordially" informing patrons that the recipes were "tested and proven by their popularity at the fair, where they were consistently preferred to the best the world had to offer." (A few of the recipes appear in this book.) In New York, where the fair's theme was "world of tomorrow," VIPs were issued wallet-sized membership cards entitling them to "the privileges of the Club Room in the

Wonder Bakery," and news flash pamphlets proclaimed the Wonder Bakery as "one of the most unique and interesting showplaces at the fair— a sight that should not be missed."

Around this time Wonder also introduced what would become a signature ad campaign. While few can forget how Wonder helped "build strong bodies," many may not recall that at first, the magic only worked eight ways (muscles, bones and teeth, body cells, blood, appetite, growth, brain, and energy). Four additional "body and brain building properties" (red cells, vitamin B_{12}, protein digestion, and tissue respiration) debuted in the 1950s.

The initial "builds strong bodies" campaign marked the beginning of a major focus on health and nutrition for the brand. In the early 1940s, Wonder became an important part of a

government-sponsored program to enrich bread with vitamins and minerals as a way of combating certain diseases. Known as the "quiet miracle," the enrichment program nearly eliminated the diseases beriberi and pellagra. A concern with nutrition has continued over the life of the product and was evidenced again years later when Wonder became the first national bread brand to feature open-dating as well as nutrition information on its packaging.

Further enhancing Wonder's wholesome image, the already popular brand became a fixture on the *Howdy Doody Show,* with the Doodyville char-

acters singing the "builds strong bodies" praises, and appeared on other family-oriented early television programs, including *The Gene Autry Show, Thunderbolt the Wonder Colt,* and *Time for Beany.*

In the late 1950s, consumers were invited to "throw away your bread box" following the introduction of cellophane-wrapped bread and the "no-tear flip seal." While shoppers bought into the new wrappers, not everything Wonder introduced was a hit. When Wonder Round sandwich bread hit the market years later, it was touted as "the best thing that ever happened to sandwiches." The idea was simple enough: round bread for round fillings, such as bologna, hamburgers, or eggs. But it didn't make the cut with consumers and was eventually discontinued.

Best thing that ever happened to sandwiches
NEW WONDER ROUND
sandwich bread!

Sandwich fillings fit neater!
From bologna to hamburgers—most fillings are round. When the bread's round—there's no waste. Every bite has filling!

Perfect for eggs and toast!
Eggs—fried or poached—fit just right! And toasting brings out all the hearty flavor and goodness in Wonder Round Bread!

Makes sense. Round bread—round filling—round sandwich. Neat. More to it than that...the special round baking pan not only changes the shape, it changes the flavor. It completely surrounds the loaf as it's baked...to keep all the goodness of Wonder where it belongs—right in the bread. Every slice gives you great new flavor from tender crust to tender center! Try new Wonder Round Sandwich Bread in every way—today!

© 1963, CONTINENTAL BAKING COMPANY, Incorporated

WONDER Round Sandwich

White Enriched Bread

helps build strong bodies 12 ways

The 1960s were an era that would have made Alice Adams Proctor blush. After years of burnishing a reputation for all-American goodness, Wonder introduced the "Helps catch boys" ad campaign, featuring such risqué headlines as "Boy Trap" and "Date Bait" over close-ups of sultry-eyed women and plump sandwiches. Some even included recipes: The Mr. Wonderful—"you'll have him eating out of your hand"; The Wonder Hero— "try this on your hero"; and The Wonder Winner—"build a better boy trap."

The history of Wonder, now owned by Interstate Bakeries Corporation, is still being written as the brand continues to evolve. More than eighty-five years after being introduced, Wonder is indelibly baked into the American consciousness—a pop culture icon that has stayed on top even in the face of food fads of every imaginable sort.

Ask around. Just about everyone has a warm Wonder memory or story to share. The following pages are filled with them from folks across the country. They speak to family, to childhood, to relationships, to friendships, to ties that bind. Tossing your first Wonder bread ball across the lunchroom might as well be a right of passage.

As Walt Harrington observed in *The Washington Post*, "The Portuguese have massa sovada bread. The Greeks have tsoureke.... But all of America...has Wonder bread."

Let the wonders never cease.

Chapter One

GOOD MORNING WONDER BREAD

Wonder Bread Eggs

This recipe was handed down to me from my grandfather, Edward Olsen, who left us with the most wonderful recipe for a quick breakfast he called stretched eggs, or, as my siblings and I called it, Wonder Bread Eggs. Grandpa Ed's recipe came about from the need to produce inexpensive, good-tasting meals. Your choices of toppings are limited only by your imagination.

RANDALL OLSEN, Kennedy, New York

Serves 2 to 3

4 large eggs

1/4 cup milk

Salt and pepper to taste

4 slices Wonder bread

2 tablespoons butter

Toppings such as maple syrup, jelly, jam, ketchup (optional)

Combine the eggs, milk, salt, and pepper in a mixing bowl. Break bread into small pieces (approximately 1-inch cubes) and add to egg mixture. Let stand for 5 minutes, stirring occasionally.

Meanwhile, melt the butter in a medium nonstick skillet over medium-high heat. Pour all of the egg-bread mixture into the hot skillet, patting down to form a pancake shape. Cook until golden brown, about 3 to 4 minutes, turn over, and cook until the other side is lightly browned. Cut in half or in thirds with a spatula. Serve with toppings, as desired.

Wonderful Bird's Nest

This recipe is particularly meaningful to me because it's the first recipe I was allowed to prepare by myself, when I was eight years old. It was a great recipe for a beginner—quick and easy but requiring some degree of culinary skill. Thanks, Wonder bread, for the memories (and for three generations of fun)!

MAY BERENBAUM, Urbana, Illinois

Serves 2

2 slices Wonder bread

2 slices cheddar or Swiss cheese

2 eggs, separated

Pinch of salt

Preheat the oven to 350°F. Spray a baking sheet with non-stick cooking spray. Place the bread on the baking sheet and top with the cheese. Put the egg whites in a mixing bowl and add the salt. Using an electric mixer on high speed or with a wire whisk, beat the egg whites until stiff peaks form. Using a large spatula, spoon the egg white mixture on top of the cheese-topped bread, forming a bird's nest shape (make a depression in the center). Carefully position 1 uncooked yolk in the central depression. Bake until the yolk sets and the egg white peaks brown slightly, about 20 minutes. Serve immediately.

Pigs in a Wonder Blanket

Pigs in a blanket are a welcome treat even on a warm summer morning. And Pigs in a Wonder Blanket, now that's one warm pig. This recipe appeared in *The Wonder Book of Good Meals*, produced for the 1934 Chicago World's Fair.

Makes 12 pigs in blankets

12 link pork sausages

6 slices Wonder bread

Melted butter, for brushing

Maple syrup or warmed tomato sauce, for serving

Fresh fruit, for serving (optional)

Preheat the oven to 425°F. Heat a skillet, and fry the sausages over medium heat until the sausages are browned and no longer pink inside; drain. Cut each slice of bread in half vertically and wrap around the sausages. Secure with toothpicks. Place in a baking dish. Brush the Wonder bread blankets lightly with melted butter. Bake for about 10 minutes to brown. Serve hot with maple syrup or warm tomato sauce, and fresh fruit, if desired.

Baked Wonder Omelet

I have used this recipe for more than forty years. This "omelet" makes it easy to serve breakfast when you have no idea what time your out-of-town guests will arrive. Just remember to put it together the night before and when they show up, pop it in the oven!

MARY KELSCH, Leesburg, Florida

Serves 6

1 (14-ounce) package
 smoked sausage links,
 cut into bite-size pieces

2 cups milk

6 eggs, lightly beaten

3/4 teaspoon dry mustard

1 teaspoon salt

1 cup shredded colby or
 cheddar cheese

1 slice Wonder bread,
 torn into pieces

Cook the sausage in a skillet over medium-high heat until browned; drain on paper towels.

Mix together the milk, eggs, dry mustard, and salt. Stir in the cheese and bread and add the sausage pieces.

Spray an 8-inch baking dish with nonstick cooking spray. Pour the mixture into the dish, cover, and refrigerate overnight.

Preheat the oven to 350°F. Bake, uncovered, for 45 minutes, or until set. Serve hot.

Apple Wonder Waffles

This recipe was originally published in *The Wonder Book of Good Meals*, which was produced for the 1934 Chicago World's Fair. It's a great way to start the day. Try it with warmed maple syrup or sausage and gravy for a real treat.

Makes 10 waffles

8 slices Wonder bread

1/2 teaspoon salt

1/3 cup butter, cut into pieces

2 cups hot milk

2 eggs

1 1/2 cups finely chopped cooking apples, such as Granny Smith or Rome

5 teaspoons baking powder

1 pound pork sausage (optional)

2 tablespoons all-purpose flour (optional)

1 cup milk (optional)

Salt and pepper to taste (optional)

Maple syrup (optional)

Preheat the oven to 300°F. Heat a waffle iron. Put the bread in a large bowl. Sprinkle with the salt and put the butter pieces on top. Pour the hot milk over. With a spoon, break the bread into pieces and stir thoroughly to combine. Beat the eggs well and stir into the bread mixture. Add the apples and baking powder and stir well to combine. Pour 1/3 to 1/2 cup of batter into the waffle iron and cook until golden brown, about 3 to 5 minutes. Carefully remove the baked waffle and place it on a baking pan in the oven to keep it warm. Repeat with the remaining batter until all is used.

To top with sausage and gravy, cook the sausage in a skillet over medium heat, stirring to crumble, until browned. Drain, reserving 2 tablespoons of the drippings. Return the drippings to the skillet over medium heat. Blend in the flour, stirring until it forms a smooth paste. Cook, stirring, for 1 minute.

• • • *continued*

• •

Gradually add the milk, stirring until smooth. Cook, stirring, until the mixture thickens and is bubbly. Stir in the cooked, drained sausage. Season to taste with salt and pepper. Serve the sausage and gravy over the waffles accompanied with maple syrup, if desired.

A Poached Egg becomes an Adventure when served on Wonder Bread toast

Place two strips of bacon between the egg and toast and you have a new breakfast delight for the whole family. The supreme goodness of Wonder Bread is at its delicious best when toasted to a golden brown —so be sure the toast is Wonder Bread and none "almost as good".

P J 301

Cinnamon Wonder Waffles

This recipe appeared in *The Wonder Book of Good Meals*, produced for the 1934 Chicago World's Fair. It's a new take on an old favorite.

Makes 12 waffles

1/3 cup butter, at room temperature, plus additional melted butter as needed for brushing

12 slices Wonder bread

3 tablespoons sugar

1 teaspoon ground cinnamon

Jelly or maple syrup, for serving

Heat a waffle iron. Spread the softened butter over one side of each slice of bread. Combine the sugar and cinnamon, then sprinkle evenly over the buttered bread. Press 2 slices together firmly, buttered sides together, to make 6 sandwiches. Cut off the crusts and cut each sandwich into halves diagonally. Brush the outsides of the sandwiches with melted butter and place 2 to 4 sandwiches (depending on the size of your waffle iron) in the waffle iron. Cook for 3 to 4 minutes, or until golden brown. Serve with jelly or maple syrup.

To use Wonder Waffles as a base for fried chicken or creamed foods, omit the sugar and cinnamon and prepare as above.

Wonder Eggs Royale

These scrumptious round sandwiches give you the pleasures of a full, hearty breakfast—eggs, bacon, and buttered, toasted Wonder bread—without all of the pans to clean. This recipe appeared in *The Wonder Book of Good Meals*, produced for the 1934 Chicago World's Fair.

Serves 4 to 6

12 slices Wonder bread

2 tablespoons butter, at room temperature

6 strips bacon

6 eggs

Salt and pepper to taste

Preheat the oven to 450°F. Using a biscuit cutter or the top of a glass, cut the bread into rounds and spread both sides with butter. Put 2 slices of buttered bread together to form 6 sandwiches. Wrap a slice of bacon tightly around the edge of each sandwich so that the bacon forms a collar extending a little above the bread. Fasten the overlapping end with a toothpick. Place the sandwiches on a baking sheet and break an egg over the center of each one. Season to taste with salt and pepper. Bake until the bacon is browned and the eggs are set, 18 to 20 minutes. Serve immediately.

Wonder Crullers

Put on a pot of coffee while these homemade sugar-coated doughnuts are being prepared, and then dip, crunch, and sip to your heart's delight. This recipe appeared in *The Wonder Book of Good Meals*, produced for the 1934 Chicago World's Fair.

Makes 3 dozen

Vegetable oil, as needed, for deep-frying

12 slices Wonder bread

2 eggs, slightly beaten

1/2 cup milk

2 tablespoons granulated sugar

1/2 teaspoon pure vanilla extract

Pinch of freshly grated nutmeg

Confectioners' sugar, for dusting

Fill a deep fryer with vegetable oil according to the manufacturer's directions, or fill a deep pan with vegetable oil to a depth of about 2 inches. Heat, uncovered, over medium heat until the oil reaches 350°F.

Cut the crusts off each slice of bread, then cut each slice into thirds. Mix together the eggs, milk, sugar, vanilla, and nutmeg in a large bowl. Dip the crullers into the mixture. Carefully place a few crullers in the hot oil (avoid over filling) and fry just until golden brown, turning the crullers with long tongs to brown evenly. Remove the crullers from the hot oil with a slotted spoon and place on a paper towel–lined plate to drain. Dust generously with confectioners' sugar and serve warm.

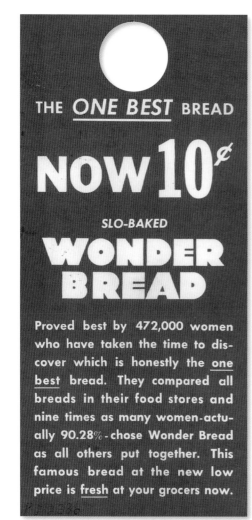

THE *ONE BEST* BREAD

NOW 10¢

SLO-BAKED

WONDER BREAD

Proved best by 472,000 women who have taken the time to discover which is honestly the <u>one best</u> bread. They compared all breads in their food stores and nine times as many women-actually 90.28%-chose Wonder Bread as all others put together. This famous bread at the new low price is <u>fresh</u> at your grocers now.

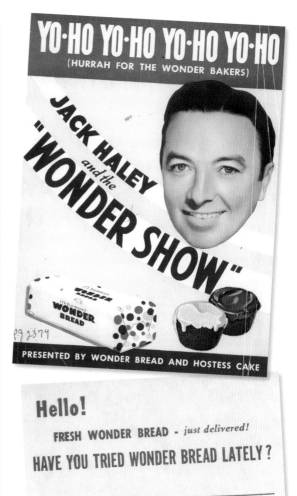

YO·HO YO·HO YO·HO YO·HO
(HURRAH FOR THE WONDER BAKERS)

JACK HALEY and the "WONDER SHOW"

WONDER BREAD

PRESENTED BY WONDER BREAD AND HOSTESS CAKE

Hello!

FRESH WONDER BREAD - *just delivered!*

HAVE YOU TRIED WONDER BREAD LATELY?

YOUR WONDER BREAD SALESMAN

Chapter Two

WONDER BITES

Wonder Blintzes

Every time I make these blintzes I get requests for copies of the recipe. This recipe can be served as a breakfast sweet, a dessert, an appetizer, or even as a side dish for lunch. I serve the blintzes with sour cream, applesauce, or fresh berries. They are also good just plain.

CARYN K. CHERPAK, Northbrook, Illinois

Makes 2 to 4 dozen

1 loaf Wonder bread,
  crusts removed

1 (8-ounce) package
  cream cheese (regular
  or reduced fat), at room
  temperature

1 egg yolk

1¹/₂ cups sugar

2 to 3 teaspoons ground
  cinnamon

¹/₂ cup unsalted butter,
  melted

Preheat the oven to 400°F. Butter an 11 by 7-inch baking dish.

Flatten each slice of bread with a rolling pin or with a drinking glass turned on its side. Using an electric mixer on medium speed, beat the cream cheese. Add the egg yolk and ¹/₂ cup of the sugar and beat just until combined. Spread the cream cheese mixture on one side of each slice of bread and roll jelly-roll fashion to make blintzes.

Combine the remaining 1 cup sugar and the cinnamon and sprinkle on a tray or sheet of waxed paper. Brush the melted butter on the blintzes and roll in the cinnamon-sugar mixture. Place in the baking dish. Bake for 13 minutes, or until golden brown. Serve warm or at room temperature.

Note: The blintzes may be prepared ahead and frozen before baking. They can also be cut in half for smaller bites. When ready to serve, thaw for 30 to 45 minutes, then bake as directed.

Wonder Cream Cheese Bites

This recipe for delicious bite-size desserts, perfect for parties and other get-togethers, has been in our family for more than twenty years. I first made it in my high school home economics class. No one can believe these sweet treats I serve on cookie trays are made from Wonder bread!

JOAN STETSER, Gibbstown, New Jersey

Makes about 3 dozen

2 loaves Wonder bread, crusts removed

1 (8-ounce) package cream cheese, at room temperature

3/4 cup sugar

2 tablespoons milk

1/2 teaspoon pure vanilla extract

Topping

1 cup sugar

2 to 3 tablespoons ground cinnamon

1/2 cup butter, melted

Roll each bread slice very thin with a rolling pin.

Using an electric mixer on high speed, beat the cream cheese until smooth. Beat in the sugar and continue beating until the mixture is light and fluffy. Add the milk and vanilla and mix well. Spread a thin layer of the cheese mixture on one side of each slice of bread. Roll each slice, jelly-roll fashion, into a log. Cut each log in half crosswise.

To make the topping, mix together the sugar and cinnamon in a small bowl. Dip each piece of the cheese log into the melted butter and then roll to cover in the cinnamon-sugar mixture. Cut in half again crosswise. Arrange on trays, seam side down. Cover and refrigerate for 1 hour, to set. Serve chilled.

Three Wonderful Pieces

This recipe has been tested for over forty years. It is kid-friendly, a good conversation starter, and, best of all, mysterious—no one knows what's in it.

MARY LOU JANTZ, Grosse Pointe Farms, Michigan

Makes 4 dozen

1/2 cup processed cheese spread

12 slices Wonder bread, crusts removed

24 strips bacon, cut in half

Preheat the oven to 400°F. Line a baking sheet with aluminum foil.

Spread about 2 tablespoons of the cheese spread over one side of each slice of bread. Cut each slice into 4 strips. Roll up each strip and wrap with half a piece of bacon. Secure with a toothpick. Place on the baking sheet, seam side down.

Bake for 25 to 30 minutes, or until the bacon is crisp, turning once halfway through. Serve warm.

Wonder Parmesan Bread

This delicious and rich recipe is a favorite among my friends. To this day, it makes my mouth water simply to read it. I always double the recipe, preparing some for the guests and some for the freezer so I can bake them up whenever I'm in the mood.

SONDRA GORDY, Conway, Arkansas

Makes about 18 stacks

1 loaf Wonder bread, crusts removed

3 eggs, beaten

1 cup butter, melted

1¹/₂ cup grated Parmesan cheese

Cut each slice of bread into 3 strips. Dip 1 strip into the beaten egg and stack it between 2 other strips, making a sandwich 3 strips high. Brush the entire stack with melted butter and then roll in the cheese, covering it completely. Arrange in an 8 by 8-inch baking dish. (The stacks can touch one another, but always be sure to keep the egg-dipped slice in the middle and the cheese-coated slices on the top and bottom.) Refrigerate for several hours or overnight.

Preheat the oven to 350°F. Bake for 10 to 15 minutes, or until golden brown. Serve warm.

Note: To freeze, cover the dish with plastic wrap or heavy-duty aluminum foil. To bake, thaw for 2 to 3 hours, then bake as directed. If you prefer to have the stacks ready to bake just a few at a time, arrange the bread stacks on a tray and freeze just until the bread stacks are firm. Then place the stacks in a zip-top bag and freeze until ready to use. To bake, arrange desired number of bread stacks on a baking sheet, allow to stand for 20 to 30 minutes, and bake as directed.

Wonder Bread Pepper Snack

- -

I lived on a small farm in the 1940s with five brothers and two sisters, and we often enjoyed this way of making a snack for ourselves. It's best with a green pepper picked fresh from the garden.

AMELIA CHAKO, Hermitage, Pennsylvania

- -

Serves 2

2 large green bell peppers

4 or 5 slices Wonder bread, smashed

Milk, as needed, to moisten the bread

2 tablespoons sugar

Cut off the top of the bell pepper and remove the seeds. Stuff the cavity with the Wonder bread. Pour milk over the stuffing to moisten and then sprinkle with the sugar. Serve.

Wonder Bread Balls

Growing up, this was a favorite snack of the neighborhood kids. It was readily available at anybody's house—we just raided the bread box!

SHARON L. TRAUDT, Northwood, Ohio

Serves 2

2 slices Wonder bread, crusts removed

Place 1 slice between the palms of your hands and roll bread into a tight ball. Proceed in this way with the next slice. Enjoy!

Wonder Asparagus Rolls to Die For

I first had these little yumettes at a dinner party and was surprised at how good they are. Anything, especially bread, brushed with butter is starting off on the right foot. I came up with a new twist by adding cheese.

CAREN ALPERT, San Francisco, California

Makes 50 to 75 pieces

25 fresh asparagus spears

Salt and pepper to taste

25 slices Wonder bread, crusts removed

1 (8-ounce) package cream cheese, at room temperature

4 ounces or about 1 cup mild blue cheese crumbles

1 egg

1 cup butter, melted

Preheat the oven to 400°F. Pour water into a large pan just to cover the asparagus; heat over high heat until boiling. Snap off and discard the woody end from the asparagus spears and add them to the boiling water. Season with salt and pepper. Partially cover the pan and cook until the asparagus are barely fork-tender, 3 to 5 minutes. Drain and then plunge into cold water to stop the cooking process. Transfer to paper towels to drain.

Slightly flatten the bread pieces with a rolling pin. Using a fork, mix together the cream cheese, blue cheese, and egg. Spread the mixture on one side of each slice of bread. Place 1 asparagus spear over the cheese mixture. Roll up the bread, jelly-roll fashion, around the asparagus. Generously brush the outside of each roll with butter, covering evenly on all sides. Slice the rolls in half or thirds and place

continued

A TRIP THROUGH A
WONDER BREAD BAKERY

on a baking sheet. Bake for 15 minutes, or until golden brown. Serve immediately.

If desired, freeze the prepared asparagus rolls before baking. To bake, place the frozen rolls on a baking sheet and bake for 15 to 20 minutes, as directed.

Variations: Here are four more ways to make these tasty rolls. (1) Add 1 cup crushed macadamia nuts to the cheese and egg mixture, then prepare as directed. (2) Add 3/4 cup grated Pecorino Romano to the cheese and egg mixture, then prepare as directed. (3) Use 12 ounces goat cheese and 3/4 cup slivered almonds instead of the cream cheese and blue cheese, add the egg, and prepare as directed. (4) Use the goat cheese filling (Variation 3), add 1 cup chopped dried apricots to the goat cheese, slivered almonds, and egg filling, then prepare the rolls without the asparagus.

Old-Fashioned Cinnamon Wonder Toast

Cinnamon toast was a real hit with my children, especially when I served it with milk or hot chocolate. I used to think children were a good excuse to have breakfasts like this. Now I just have breakfasts like this anyway.

REGINA POWELL, Lansdowne, Pennsylvania

Serves 2

2 tablespoons butter,
  at room temperature

2 slices Wonder bread

2 teaspoons ground
  cinnamon

1 teaspoon sugar

Butter one side of each slice of bread. Place the bread buttered side up on a baking sheet or broiler pan. Mix together the cinnamon and sugar and sprinkle onto the buttered bread. Broil the bread 4 inches from the heat until golden brown. Serve warm.

Wonder Beef Cups

This recipe is from the Wonder archives. It's been around for a long time, and for good reason—it's great for a lunch or dinner dish.

Serves 6

3 tablespoons butter,
  at room temperature

12 slices Wonder bread

1 1/4 pounds ground beef

1 egg

1 small onion, chopped

1 (10 3/4-ounce) can cream
  of mushroom soup

Salt and pepper to taste

3/4 cup shredded cheddar
  cheese

Preheat the oven to 350°F. Butter one side of each slice of Wonder bread and press each slice butter side down into the cups of a muffin tin. In a medium bowl, mix together the ground beef, egg, onion, soup, salt, and pepper until well blended. Fill each bread cup with the mixture. Sprinkle shredded cheddar cheese over the top.

Bake for 30 minutes, or until the meat is cooked through. Gently lift out of the muffin tins and serve immediately.

Chapter Three

WONDER SANDWICHES

Grilled Peanut Butter, Jelly, and Wonder

• •

My mom used to make these every Sunday evening. Now I make them often, too. They're "snackably" good.

RUTH AND BUCK GILPIN, Sterling, Pennsylvania

• •

Serves 2

4 slices Wonder bread

4 tablespoons peanut butter

2 tablespoons grape jelly

2 tablespoons butter, at room temperature

Spread one side of each slice of bread with peanut butter and then spread with jelly. Assemble the sandwiches with the peanut butter and jelly inside. Spread the outside of the sandwiches with butter.

Heat a large skillet or griddle over medium-high heat. Fry the sandwiches until golden on one side, 2 to 4 minutes, then turn and cook until golden on the other side. Allow to cool slightly before serving.

Wonder Chip "Wich"

When I was a child, I didn't like regular sandwiches. My mother had the solution: she made potato chip sandwiches for my school lunches. Forty years later, I still enjoy the chip "wich."

NANCY OSTROWSKI, Alexandria, Virginia

Serves 2

4 teaspoons mayonnaise

4 slices Wonder bread

12 to 14 potato chips

Spread mayonnaise on one side of each slice of bread. Top 1 slice with chips and then top with a second slice of bread, mayonnaise side down.

IT'S NEW! IT'S SMART!
WONDER THIN SLICED BREAD
FOR DAINTY DELICIOUS SANDWICHES

Grilled Baloney and Wonder

I grew up in a large family and we ate Wonder bread almost every day. My parents even went to the Wonder bread bakery to get the freshest loaves. This recipe in particular has been a family favorite—it's delicious and easy to make.

PATTY FRANCO ROBERGE, Bloomfield Hills, Michigan

Serves 2

2 tablespoons butter

2 slices bologna

4 slices Wonder bread

2 tablespoons mayonnaise

Melt the butter in a large skillet over medium-high heat. Cut a slit about 1 inch long in the center of the bologna. Fry the bologna for 2 to 3 minutes on each side, or until browned and hot.

Spread one side of each slice of Wonder bread with mayonnaise. Place the hot bologna on top of 1 slice of bread and cover with second slice of bread, mayonnaise side down.

Wonder Omelet Sandwiches

This is great for big eaters because it's substantial, but easy to make. It's also perfect for brunches, and it's easy to serve since you prepare it the night before. Your guests will be asking you for the recipe.

SUE ROSS, Casa Grande, Arizona

Serves 8

4 to 6 tablespoons butter, at room temperature, plus 1/2 cup butter or margarine, melted

16 slices Wonder bread

8 slices cheddar, American, or Swiss cheese

8 thin slices cooked ham

6 eggs

3 cups milk

1/2 teaspoon dry mustard

Salt to taste

1 cup crushed cornflakes or potato chips

Lightly butter one side of each slice of bread. Top 8 slices of buttered bread with a slice of cheese and a slice of ham. Top with a second slice of bread, buttered side down. Arrange the sandwiches in a greased 12 by 18-inch open roasting pan or 11 1/2 by 17-inch jelly-roll pan.

Whisk together the eggs, milk, mustard, and salt and pour slowly over the sandwiches. Cover and refrigerate overnight.

Preheat the oven to 350°F. Mix together the cornflake crumbs and melted butter; sprinkle over the top of the sandwiches. Bake uncovered for 1 hour, or until golden brown.

Wonder Sausage and Peppers

Growing up in the early 1960s, I carried my lunch to school every day—a meal made by my Italian mom with culinary influence from my Syrian dad. A favorite treat combined both of their cultures: sausage and pepper sandwiches in pita bread. Schoolmates would often ask: "What kind of sandwich is that?" or "We never saw bread like that," and I'd go home crying. Wonder bread (and my mom) came to the rescue.

WEDA MOSELLIE, Phillipsburg, New Jersey

Serves 2

3 Italian hot sausage links

1 tablespoon olive oil

1 red bell pepper, cut into strips

1 red onion, chopped

1 (4-ounce) can sliced mushrooms, drained

4 slices Wonder bread

Put the sausages in a saucepan and cover with water. Boil for 5 minutes and then drain. Heat the oil in a large skillet. Add the sausages and cook, turning to brown evenly, for 10 minutes, or until they are no longer pink inside. Remove the sausages and keep warm. Add the red pepper and onion, and cook, stirring, until the vegetables are tender. Stir in the mushrooms and cook for 3 to 4 minutes longer.

Slice the sausage links in half lengthwise. Place the sausages and vegetables on 2 slices of bread; top each with a second slice of bread.

Note: Wrap the sandwiches in aluminum foil. When ready to serve, use the foil as a "plate" for the sandwich.

Wonder Trail Mix Sandwich

One day my granddaughter wanted something sweet for lunch and I hadn't been to the store yet. So the two of us concocted this sandwich, which is delicious and healthy, and satisfied her craving for something sweet.

CAROLYN TORRANCE, Ripley, New York

Serves 2

4 slices Wonder bread, toasted

6 tablespoons crunchy peanut butter

2 ripe bananas, sliced

2 tablespoons raisins

2 teaspoons chopped cashews

2 teaspoons honey

Spread one side of 2 pieces of toast with peanut butter. Place the banana slices on top of the other 2 slices of toast. Top the banana with raisins and cashews, then drizzle with honey. Top with the second slices of toast, peanut butter side down.

Wonder Kid Sandwiches

Kids may be the best audience for these fun and easy sandwiches, but they aren't the only ones who can enjoy them. "Kids" of all ages find them delicious, as they have since the recipe appeared in *The Wonder Book of Good Meals*, produced for the 1934 Chicago World's Fair.

Makes 1 to 2 dozen

Cookie cutters in fun shapes such as bears, rabbits, or hearts

12 slices Wonder bread

3 tablespoons butter, at room temperature

2 tablespoons sugar

1 teaspoon ground cinnamon

With the cookie cutters, cut shapes from the slices of Wonder bread, avoiding the crust. Spread one side of each shape with butter. Place buttered side up on a baking sheet. Combine the sugar and cinnamon and sprinkle evenly over the shapes. Broil until toasted and golden brown.

Variations: Substitute cheese and paprika for the sugar and cinnamon and toast in the broiler. Or, first toast the shapes and then spread with jam, peanut butter, cream cheese, frosting, candy sprinkles, or other sweet toppings.

Chapter Four

BAKED WONDER

A Perfectly Wonderful Casserole

This recipe is an ideal brunch main course because everyone loves it. You can make it ahead of time, too, which is always a bonus when you're serving a group.

JO-ANNE DOBRICK, Chicago, Illinois

Serves 8 to 10

2 well-beaten eggs

2¹/₂ cups milk

1 teaspoon dry mustard

1 teaspoon garlic salt

Salt and pepper to taste

1 loaf Wonder bread, crusts removed

¹/₂ cup butter, melted

2 cups shredded sharp cheddar cheese

1 (10³/₄-ounce) can cream of mushroom soup (optional)

¹/₂ cup milk (optional)

1 cup salsa (optional)

Mix together the eggs, milk, dry mustard, garlic salt, and salt and pepper. Cut each slice of bread in half diagonally and dip into the melted butter. Arrange the bread in an overlapping layer in a 9 by 13-inch baking dish; sprinkle with some of the cheese. Repeat with 2 more overlapping layers of bread and cheese. Pour the eggs mixture over the top. Cover and refrigerate overnight.

Preheat the oven to 350°F. Bake for 1¹/₂ hours, or until set. Sprinkle some more cheese over the top and allow it to melt before removing the casserole from the oven.

Combine the cream of mushroom soup and milk in a small saucepan. Heat over low heat, stirring, until hot. Serve the casserole with the mushroom sauce or salsa on the side, if desired.

Sweetened Tomato and Wonder Casserole

I've been making this recipe since I was twelve years old. My mom created this nutritious, economical, and delicious dish because she had eight children and lived on a farm.

LEAH PEKLO, Farmington Hills, Michigan

Serves 8 to 10

1/2 cup butter, at room temperature

1 loaf Wonder bread

2 (28-ounce) cans whole tomatoes

Pinch of salt

2 tablespoons sugar, or to taste

Lightly butter one side of each slice of bread. Preheat the oven to 350°F.

Combine the tomatoes, salt, and sugar in a small saucepan over medium heat. Bring to a boil, lower the heat, and simmer for 10 to 15 minutes. Spoon about one-third of the hot tomato mixture into a 9 by 13-inch baking dish. Arrange about one-third of the bread over the top. Repeat with 2 more layers of tomatoes and bread. Bake for 30 minutes, or until hot and the top is golden brown. Serve immediately.

Wonderfully Crunchy Chicken Casserole

This serves quite a few people and comes in handy when you don't know how many to expect. (Family members often do that to you.) Put it together the night before, then pop it in the oven an hour and a half before dinnertime.

LEAH PEKLO, Farmington Hills, Michigan

Serves 9 to 12

6 to 8 tablespoons butter, at room temperature

2 cups sliced fresh mushrooms

8 slices Wonder bread

2 to 3 cups chopped cooked chicken

1 (8-ounce) can sliced water chestnuts, drained

8 slices sharp cheddar cheese

1 cup mayonnaise

4 eggs, lightly beaten

1 ($10^3/4$-ounce) can cream of celery soup

1 ($10^3/4$-ounce) can cream of mushroom soup

$1^1/2$ cups milk

$1/2$ teaspoon salt

Melt 2 tablespoons of the butter in a small skillet over medium-high heat. Add the mushrooms and cook, stirring occasionally, until tender; set aside.

Butter both sides of the bread. Arrange in a 9 by 13-inch baking dish, cutting to fit as necessary. Cover the bread with the mushrooms, chicken, water chestnuts, and cheese.

Mix together the mayonnaise, eggs, celery and mushroom soups, milk, and salt; pour the mixture over the casserole. Cover and refrigerate overnight.

Preheat the oven to 350°F. Bake for $1^1/2$ hours, or until set and golden brown.

Tropical Wonder Casserole

· ·

My mom makes a version of this casserole with only the pineapple, and it's a big hit with our family at Easter as a side dish to the baked ham. The pineapple adds a tropical flavor and together with the pears and apples makes this a good side dish for other meats as well, like roast pork, pork chops, or chicken.

LAUREN SANTULLO, Berkeley Heights, New Jersey

· ·

Serves 8

4 eggs

1/2 cup sugar

1 (20-ounce) can crushed pineapple, drained

1/2 cup peeled, chopped apples

1/2 cup peeled, chopped pears

1 tablespoon raisins

1/2 cup butter, cut into pieces

4 slices Wonder bread, torn into bite-size pieces

Ground cinnamon

Preheat the oven to 350°F. Place the eggs in a large mixing bowl and beat lightly. Stir in the sugar. Stir in the pineapple, apples, pears, raisins, and butter. Gently stir in the bread. Spoon into a lightly greased 9 by 13-inch baking dish. Sprinkle the top with cinnamon. Bake uncovered for 45 to 60 minutes, or until golden and set. Allow to cool for 15 minutes before serving.

Chapter Five

SWEET AND FRUITY WONDER

The Most Wonderful Apple Pie Squares

Several years ago I invited some guests for dinner. When I discovered I had no flour to make my apple pie crust, I improvised with a loaf of Wonder bread. Whenever I prepare this recipe it brings back happy memories.

GLORIA T. BOVE, Bethlehem, Pennsylvania

Serves 10

1 cup granulated sugar

1 teaspoon ground cinnamon

4 to 6 apples, peeled and thinly sliced (10 cups)

1/2 cup golden raisins

1 cup chopped walnuts

1 teaspoon grated lemon zest

10 slices Wonder bread, crusts removed

2 large eggs

1/2 cup unsalted butter, melted

1 teaspoon pure vanilla extract

1/4 cup confectioners' sugar, for dusting (optional)

Ice cream, for serving (optional)

Preheat the oven to 350°F. Butter a 9 by 13-inch baking dish.

Combine the sugar and cinnamon and measure out 1/4 cup of it. Set the remaining cinnamon-sugar aside.

Place the apples in a large mixing bowl. Sprinkle with the 1/4 cup cinnamon-sugar. Add the raisins, half of the walnuts, and the lemon zest; gently toss to coat the apples. Spoon into the baking dish. Arrange the bread slices in a single layer over the fruit mixture, cutting to fit as necessary.

In a medium mixing bowl, beat the eggs. Add the butter, vanilla, and remaining 3/4 cup cinnamon-sugar; mix well. Spoon the mixture evenly over the bread. Sprinkle the remaining 1/2 cup walnuts over everything. Bake for 45 to 55 minutes, or until golden brown. Dust with confectioners' sugar and serve warm, with ice cream, if desired.

Wonder Pear Cobbler

• •

I love pears and I freeze them every year. Searching for a new way to use them, I created this cobbler using Wonder bread as the crust. I've been eating my pears this way ever since.

MARY LEE WRIGHT, Vardaman, Mississippi

• •

Serves 9 to 12

6 slices Wonder bread, crusts removed

4 cups frozen pears, including juice

1¹/₂ cups sugar

2 tablespoons all-purpose flour

1 egg, beaten

¹/₂ cup butter or margarine, melted

¹/₄ cup milk

Preheat the oven to 350°F. Cut the bread slices into strips. Place the pears and their juice in a 9 by 13-inch baking dish. Place the strips of bread over the pears. In a bowl, mix together the sugar, flour, egg, butter, and milk to blend well. Pour the mixture over the strips of bread. Bake for 35 to 40 minutes, or until golden. Serve warm.

All-American Peach Pie Wonder

Savor the sweetness of summer with this wonderful take on an all-American classic.

Serves 12

5 slices Wonder bread,
  crusts removed

6 fresh peaches, peeled,
  pitted, and sliced

1/2 cup butter, softened

1 1/2 cups sugar

2 tablespoons all-purpose
  flour

1 egg

Preheat the oven to 350°F. Butter an 8-inch square baking dish. Cut each Wonder bread slice into 4 or 5 strips. Spread the fruit in the baking pan and cover with a layer of bread strips. In a separate mixing bowl, beat together the butter, sugar, flour, and egg. Gently spread over the fruit and bread. Bake 40 to 50 minutes, or until golden brown.

Wonderstrudel

I came up with this recipe because strudel is popular in our family and while I like to bake, I hate to deal with pastry dough. I remembered that when I was little, I would squish my sandwich bread. I thought that if you can squish the bread in a sandwich, you could just flatten it out and make a pastry dough. I tried it, and it worked.

HANNAH LESKOSKY, Urbana, Illinois

Serves 8

1 cup peeled, chopped apples

2 tablespoons grape juice

$1/4$ cup brown sugar

$1^1/2$ teaspoons ground cinnamon, plus more for topping

$1/8$ teaspoon ground nutmeg

$1/3$ cup chopped almonds, toasted

12 slices Wonder bread, crusts removed

3 to 4 tablespoons butter, melted

Whipped cream, for serving (optional)

Preheat the oven to 350°F. Combine the apples and grape juice; set aside and allow to stand for about 5 minutes.

Combine the brown sugar, $1^1/2$ teaspoons of the cinnamon, the nutmeg, and almonds.

Put 2 slices of the bread side by side and roll together until the bread is quite thin and the pieces stick together to form a sheet. Repeat with the remaining bread, making a total of 6 thin "sheets" of bread.

Carefully transfer one sheet to a lightly greased 11 by 7-inch baking pan. Brush the top of the bread with melted butter. Sprinkle with about $1^1/2$ to 2 tablespoons of the sugar-almond mixture. Top with another sheet of bread, brush with butter, and sprinkle with more of the sugar-almond mixture. Top with a third sheet of bread, brush with butter, and sprinkle with some of the sugar-almond

• • • continued

mixture. Top this with about half of the chopped apples. Repeat with 2 more "sheets" of 2 slices of bread, spreading each with butter and sprinkling with the sugar-almond mixture. Spoon the remaining apples on top. Finish the strudel with the last "sheet" of bread and brush the top generously with the remaining butter. Sprinkle the top of the strudel with cinnamon. Bake for 25 to 30 minutes, or until golden brown and the apples are tender. Allow to cool slightly and then slice into pieces. Garnish each piece with whipped cream, if desired.

Wonderful Napoleon

I've always been known for finding innovative ways to make classic desserts. Napoleons are a favorite of mine, and Wonder bread seemed like the perfect substitute for puff pastry, providing a good balance in taste when topped with the sweet strawberries and cream.

EDWARD DUBROSKI, Clark, New Jersey

Serves 2

6 slices Wonder bread

2 tablespoons butter, at room temperature

$1/2$ cup granulated sugar

2 cups heavy whipping cream

1 cup prepared vanilla pudding (canned, purchased, or home-made)

2 cups fresh strawberries

Confectioners' sugar, for dusting (optional)

Chocolate syrup, for serving (optional)

Strawberry sauce, for serving (optional)

Cut a circle from each slice of bread using a biscuit cutter or the top of a glass. Brush each round slice with a teaspoon of butter and sprinkle each with a teaspoon of the granulated sugar. Toast each round in a toaster oven or under the broiler until golden brown; set aside to cool.

Beat the cream with an electric mixer on high speed or with a wire whisk until frothy and stiff peaks form. Gradually add the remaining granulated sugar, and continue to beat until stiff peaks form. Divide the stiffly beaten cream in half; cover and refrigerate half for use as a topping. Add half of the whipped cream to the vanilla pudding, folding until fully incorporated. (Refrigerate for up to 1 hour if not assembling immediately.) Slice the strawberries in half lengthwise.

To assemble the napoleon, put one of the toasted bread rounds on a serving plate. (Use a small spoonful

• • • continued

of vanilla pudding mixture under the bread round to secure
it.) Top the bread round with 2 tablespoons of the pudding
mixture. Put a few strawberry halves on the pudding. Put
another bread round on the strawberries. Top with 2 tablespoons of the pudding mixture and some of the strawberries.
Add a dollop of the whipped cream. Top the cream with the
third bread round. Sift confectioner's sugar over the bread,
if desired, and garnish the plate with the remaining fresh
strawberries and whipped cream. Drizzle the chocolate and
strawberry sauces around the plate in decorative fashion, if
desired. Repeat for the second napolean, and enjoy.

ENTRY BLA

$2000.⁰⁰   WORLD'S FAIR
WONDER BREAD CONTEST
25,210 VALUABLE PRIZES GIVEN AWAY
FIRST PRIZE $500—2 SECOND PRIZES $75 EACH—7 THIRD PRIZES $50 EACH—200 FOURTH PRIZES $5 EACH
25,000 CONSOLATION PRIZES of one key giving you an opportunity to get a free automobile in the Golden Key Contest at the World's Fair
HERE'S WHAT YOU DO — Write in the space provided, in twenty-five words or less, why you are convinced that WONDER BREAD
is actually the one *best* bread. Fill in your name and the address of your grocer and leave this card at your grocer's the next time you call.
The WONDER BREAD salesman will pick it up and enter you in the contest.
——— PRINT YOUR MESSAGE HERE PLAINLY ———

NAME ....   GROCER'S NAME ....
ADDRESS ....   ADDRESS ....   (Se   e)
This contest is not open to employees of Continental Baking Company. In case of ties, equal prizes will be awarded.

Wonder Easter Egg Sandwich

· ·

This sandwich was "invented" by my father, John E. Addis, when he was a boy. I enjoyed it as a child every Easter and have passed it along to my children. It's a family tradition.

DAVID ADDIS, Chesterfield, New Jersey

· ·

Serves 2

2 tablespoons butter,
    at room temperature

4 slices Wonder bread

2 (1-ounce) chocolate-
    covered coconut eggs,
    sliced, or several slices,
    as desired, from larger
    candy eggs

Liberally butter one side of each slice of bread. Put half of the chocolate egg slices on one slice of the buttered bread and top with a second slice of bread, buttered side down. Repeat for the second sandwich.

WONDER BREAD PUDDING AND CRÊPES

Top-of-the-Morning Wonder Bread Pudding

This is a twist on a recipe I saw in a newspaper and have been making for more than twenty years. Don't be surprised when the pudding shrinks somewhat after it is removed from the oven. Nothing is lost: Pour a little cold heavy cream over the warm pudding, and you'll be in heaven.

LUCY KARNEK, Burgettstown, Pennsylvania

Serves 4 to 6

1 large egg

¹/₄ cup sugar

2 cups milk

1 teaspoon pure vanilla extract

¹/₂ teaspoon ground cinnamon

¹/₈ teaspoon salt

5 slices day-old Wonder bread, cut into cubes

¹/₄ cup raisins

Ground nutmeg

Heavy whipping cream, for serving (optional)

Preheat the oven to 350°F. Lightly butter an 8 by 8-inch baking dish.

Combine the egg, sugar, milk, vanilla, cinnamon, and salt in a large mixing bowl; beat well. Add the bread cubes and raisins and mix well. Pour into the prepared dish. Sprinkle the top with nutmeg. Bake, uncovered, for 1 hour, or until golden brown, the top puffs, and a knife inserted into the center comes out clean. Spoon on to plates and serve warm. If desired, pour a little heavy whipping cream over the top of each piece just before serving.

Wonderful Crêpes Suzette

As a child, I spent several summers going to Boy Scout camp. The food was terrible—except when we were able to "borrow" loaves of Wonder bread and fresh fruit to make our own meals. The combination of fruit and Wonder bread became our staple snack every summer. I've taken that memory and turned it into this gourmet dessert.

NOLAN STUDLEY, New York, New York

Serves 8

8 slices Wonder bread, crusts removed

10 tablespoons butter, softened

2 tablespoons sugar

3 tablespoons freshly squeezed orange juice

2 tablespoons freshly squeezed lemon juice

Grated zest of 1 orange

Grated zest of 1 lemon

2 tablespoons orange marmalade

Vanilla or orange creamsicle ice cream

Orange slices, for serving

Using a rolling pin or tall drinking glass, roll each slice of bread until the slice is as thin as a crêpe. Butter one side of each slice of bread with 6 tablespoons of the butter. Sprinkle the sugar evenly over the butter on each slice. Fold each slice over diagonally and then diagonally again to create a small triangular crêpe. Butter and sugar each side of the triangular crêpes using 2 tablespoons of the butter.

In a large nonstick skillet, melt the remaining 2 tablespoons butter over low heat. Add the juices, fruit zests, and marmalade. Stir to combine and simmer for 2 to 3 minutes. Carefully place the crêpes in the skillet and ladle the mixture over the crêpes until well coated. Spoon into serving dishes and accompany each with a scoop of ice cream. Garnish with the orange slices.

continued

• •

Variation: If desired, flambé with brandy, Grand Marnier, or Cointreau. To flambé, add 4 tablespoons of the liqueur to the juice and marmalade mixture before adding the crêpes. Carefully light the liqueur. When the flame subsides, add the crêpes to the skillet. Ladle the mixture over the crêpes until well coated and serve as directed above.

Wonder Caramel Apple Bread Pudding

One of the first things I cooked after getting married was a bread pudding made with Wonder bread. It is so easy. I now make several kinds of bread pudding but this recipe, based on my mom's creation, is our favorite.

CAMMIE GRISWOLD, Leesburg, Florida

Serves 6

4 slices Wonder bread,
  cut into cubes (3 cups)

3 cups peeled, sliced
  apples

4 eggs, well beaten

1 1/2 cups milk

3 tablespoons sugar

1/2 teaspoon pure vanilla
  extract

Pinch of salt

1/4 teaspoon ground
  cinnamon

1/3 cup caramel ice cream
  topping, plus more for
  serving

Ground nutmeg

Preheat the oven to 350°F. Place the bread cubes in a buttered 8 by 8-inch dish. Top with the apple slices. Beat together the eggs, milk, sugar, vanilla, salt, and cinnamon. Pour over the apples. Drizzle with the caramel topping. Sprinkle with the nutmeg. Place the filled dish in a 9 by 13-inch glass baking dish. Pour water to a depth of 1 inch into the larger dish. Bake for 1 hour, or until a knife inserted into the center comes out clean. Drizzle with more caramel topping before serving.

Grandma's Wonder Bread Pudding with Lemon Sauce

My grandmother made this recipe often when I was growing up, and it was a favorite of mine. I've turned it into a continuing family favorite. The lemon sauce adds pizzazz.

SUE ROSS, Casa Grande, Arizona

Serves 6 to 8

6 to 8 slices Wonder bread, torn into 1/2-inch pieces

1/4 cup raisins

Pudding
3 cups milk

7 large eggs

3/4 cup sugar

1/2 teaspoon pure vanilla extract

Lemon Sauce
3/4 cup sugar

1/2 cup freshly squeezed lemon juice

2 tablespoons cornstarch

1 tablespoon plus 1 1/2 teaspoons water

4 drops yellow food coloring (optional)

Preheat the oven to 350°F. Place the bread in a buttered 2-quart casserole dish. Sprinkle with the raisins. To make the pudding, mix together the milk, eggs, sugar, and vanilla; pour over the bread and raisins. Bake, uncovered, for 1 hour, or until a knife inserted into the center comes out clean.

Meanwhile, make the lemon sauce. Combine the sugar and lemon juice in a small saucepan. Heat to a boil over medium heat. In a small bowl, combine the cornstarch and water, blending until completely smooth. Stir in the food coloring, if desired. Stir the cornstarch mixture into the boiling lemon juice. Cook, stirring constantly, until the mixture thickens and bubbles, about 5 minutes.

Cut the bread pudding into squares. Serve the warm lemon sauce spooned over the warm bread pudding.

Wonder Apricot Pudding

This recipe appeared in *The Wonder Book of Good Meals*, produced for the 1934 Chicago World's Fair. This dessert is especially tasty served with cream, hard sauce, or some of the juice from the apricots. Hard sauce is made by beating butter, granulated or confectioners' sugar, and brandy, rum, or whiskey, or vanilla or other extracts, together. The mixture is refrigerated until it becomes "hard," or the texture of butter.

Serves 6

1/2 cup butter, softened

18 slices Wonder bread

2 (15 1/4-ounce cans) apricot halves, drained with liquid reserved

1/3 cup sugar

Heavy whipping cream, hard sauce, or reserved apricot juice, for serving (optional)

Preheat the oven to 400°F. Place 1 tablespoon of the butter in each of 6 (6-ounce) custard cups. Microwave on high power for 30 to 60 seconds, or until the butter is melted.

Cut a round from each slice of bread using a 3-inch cutter. Spread the remaining 2 tablespoons butter on one side of each round of bread. Set 6 apricot halves aside and leave whole. Coarsely chop the remaining apricots, then mash with a fork. Put 1 apricot half, cut side down, in each custard cup. Top each apricot with 1 buttered round of bread, buttered side up. Put 1 round teaspoonful of mashed apricot on the bread and sprinkle with some of the sugar. Cover with a second round of buttered bread, another teaspoon of mashed apricot, and more of the sugar, and top with a third round of bread, buttered side up. Place the filled custard cups on baking sheets. Bake for 10 minutes and remove from the oven. Let set for 20 minutes, then unmold each custard onto a serving plate. Serve warm.

World's fairs are known for bringing together a cornucopia of flavors, cultures, and customs. But when it came to food at the 1934 Chicago World's Fair, some of the most unusual recipes may have been found in *The Wonder Book of Good Meals,* which was printed especially for the occasion.

This chapter includes a few of the wackier *Good Meals* recipes, as well as examples of far-out vintage fare from other promotional materials distributed by the bakers of Wonder over the years. The recipes appear just as they did originally—they have not been updated to reflect modern techniques or food trends. Take a look; it's a wonder how times have changed.

Chapter Seven

IT'S A WONDER

Pilgrim Pies

From *The Wonder Book of Good Meals*, 1934 Chicago World's Fair Edition

Serves 6

2 cups cold [fully cooked]
   minced lamb

1 tablespoon minced
   parsley

1 tablespoon Worcester-
   shire sauce

Salt and pepper

1 cup lamb gravy,
   thickened

6 slices Wonder bread,
   buttered

3 cups freshly mashed
   potatoes

2 tablespoons butter

Paprika

Preheat oven to 475°F. Combine the lamb, parsley, season-ing, and gravy. Spread portions on each of the slices of bread. Cover each lightly with a mound of mashed potato, dot with butter, and sprinkle with paprika. Place on a baking sheet and brown quickly in the oven for about 10 minutes.

De Luxe Bridge Loaf

From *The Wonder Book of Good Meals*, 1934 Chicago World's Fair Edition

Serves 8

16 slices Wonder bread

Butter

2 cups minced ham

2 hard-cooked eggs, chopped

1/2 teaspoon minced onion

Mayonnaise

1/2 pound [8 ounces] cream cheese

Cream

Paprika

Lettuce leaves, for serving

Olives, for serving

Remove the crusts from the bread and spread with butter. Mix the ham, eggs, and onion with sufficient mayonnaise to bind mixture together. Spread a portion of mixture on each slice of bread, placing one slice on top of another in a pile. Press gently together and lay the stack on a waxed paper. Wrap firmly and place in refrigerator to chill.

Slightly thin the cream cheese with sufficient cream to beat fluffy. When ready to serve, unwrap the loaf, coat with the beaten cheese, sprinkle with paprika, and garnish with lettuce and olives. To serve, cut in slices on the bias.

Swedish Pork Chops

From *The Wonder Book of Good Meals*, 1934 Chicago World's Fair Edition

Serves 6

8 slices Wonder bread

1 1/2 cups peeled and sliced apples

1/2 cup sliced apples, peels on

1/2 cup sliced onions

Salt and pepper

6 pork chops

Preheat the oven to 375°F. Break the bread into small pieces. Put in a greased covered baker. Cover bread with a layer of apples, a layer of onions, and season with salt and pepper. Place the chops on top and season. Bake, covered, in a moderate oven for 45 minutes. Uncover and brown.

Jellied Eggs

From a vintage pamphlet titled *New Wonders for Menus*

Serves 4

1 tablespoon granulated
  gelatin

2 tablespoons cold water

Salt and pepper

1/2 teaspoon minced onion

2 tablespoons vinegar

1 cup hot clear meat stock

4 eggs (poached and
  cooled)

4 slices Wonder bread, cut
  into rounds

4 small lettuce leaves,
  for serving

Vegetable salad,
  for serving

Soak the gelatin in the cold water. Add the seasoning, onion, vinegar, and hot stock. Thoroughly chill. When about to set, put two tablespoons of the mixture in each of four small sauce dishes. Turn one egg, top down, in each dish. Cover with the remaining gelatin mixture. Place in refrigerator to set. Unmold on rounds of buttered Wonder bread. Garnish with a lettuce leaf filled with vegetable salad.

Creamed Fish in Wonder Patty Shells

From *The Wonder Book of Good Meals*, 1934 Chicago World's Fair Edition

Serves 6

18 slices Wonder bread

Butter

3 cups well-seasoned
   creamed fish

Chopped mustard pickle,
   for serving

Preheat the oven to 475°F. Cut large rounds from each slice of bread. Butter 6 of the rounds. Cut 12 small rounds from the remaining 12 large rounds, leaving 12 rings. Make sandwiches of the 12 rings and place 1 sandwich ring on each of the 6 buttered rounds to make a patty. Brush all with melted butter. Brush the 12 small rounds with melted butter also.

Place the patties and small rounds on a pan in the oven and bake until golden brown. Remove to a warm platter, fill the patties with thoroughly heated fish and cap each with one of the small rounds. Garnish with the remaining rounds spread with chopped mustard pickle.

Mrs. Proctor's Devilled Crab

· ·

From *The Wonder Book of Good Meals*, 1934 Chicago World's Fair Edition

· ·

Serves 6

1/4 cup butter

8 slices Wonder bread

1/2 cup cream or evaporated milk

1 1/2 cups flaked crab meat (with liquor)

Salt and pepper

1/2 teaspoon prepared mustard

1 teaspoon Worcestershire sauce

Paprika

Preheat the oven to 425°F. Butter 6 slices of bread and place on a greased baking sheet. Break the remaining 2 slices of bread in small pieces. Pour cream or milk over the broken bread; work with a fork and add crab and seasoning. Mix well and heap a portion on the buttered slices of bread. Dot with remaining butter and sprinkle generously with paprika. Bake until brown, about 15 minutes.

Delicious Lenten Pudding

From an Alice Adams Proctor pamphlet titled *New Suggestions for Lenten Dishes*

Serves 6

6 slices buttered Wonder

1 cup apple sauce

1 glass tart jelly

1 banana

¹/₄ pound marshmallows

Preheat the oven to 350°F. Cover the bottom of a buttered baking dish with buttered Wonder bread. Cover with a mixture of apple sauce, jelly, mashed banana, and cut up marshmallows. Cover with slices of buttered Wonder bread. Bake in a moderate oven for 25 minutes. Top with marshmallows. Return to the oven to brown. Serve hot or cold.

LATEST SPOT NEWS FROM THE WONDER BAKERY AT THE WORLD'S FAIR!!

Index

● ● **A** ● ●

All-American Peach Pie Wonder, 67
Almonds
    Wonderstrudel, 69–70
Apples
    Apple Wonder Waffles, 19–20
    Delicious Lenten Pudding, 95
    The Most Wonderful Apple Pie
        Squares, 64
    Swedish Pork Chops, 90
    Tropical Wonder Casserole, 60
    Wonder Caramel Apple Bread
        Pudding, 82
    Wonderstrudel, 69–70
Apricot Pudding, Wonder, 85
Asparagus Rolls to Die For, Wonder, 36–38

● ● **B** ● ●

Bacon
    Three Wonderful Pieces, 31
    Wonder Eggs Royale, 23
Baked Wonder Omelet, 18
Balls, Wonder Bread, 35
Baloney and Wonder, Grilled, 47
Bananas
    Delicious Lenten Pudding, 95
    Wonder Trail Mix Sandwich, 51

Beef Cups, Wonder, 41
Bird's Nest, Wonderful, 15
Blintzes, Wonder, 28
Breakfast
    Apple Wonder Waffles, 19–20
    Baked Wonder Omelet, 18
    Cinnamon Wonder Waffles, 22
    Old-Fashioned Cinnamon Wonder
        Toast, 39
    Pigs in a Wonder Blanket, 17
    Top-of-the-Morning Wonder Bread
        Pudding, 78
    Wonder Blintzes, 28
    Wonder Bread Eggs, 14
    Wonder Crullers, 25
    Wonder Eggs Royale, 23
    Wonderful Bird's Nest, 15
    Wonder Omelet Sandwiches, 49

● ● **C** ● ●

Casseroles
    A Perfectly Wonderful Casserole, 57
    Sweetened Tomato and Wonder
        Casserole, 58
    Tropical Wonder Casserole, 60
    Wonderfully Crunchy Chicken
        Casserole, 59

Cheese
    Baked Wonder Omelet, 18
    De Luxe Bridge Loaf, 89
    A Perfectly Wonderful Casserole, 57
    Three Wonderful Pieces, 31
    Wonder Asparagus Rolls to Die For,
        36–38
    Wonder Beef Cups, 41
    Wonder Blintzes, 28
    Wonder Cream Cheese Bites, 30
    Wonderful Bird's Nest, 15
    Wonderfully Crunchy Chicken
        Casserole, 59
    Wonder Omelet Sandwiches, 49
    Wonder Parmesan Bread, 33
Chicago World's Fair, 6, 86
Chicken Casserole, Wonderfully Crunchy,
    59
Chocolate
    Wonder Easter Egg Sandwich, 74
    Cinnamon Wonder Toast, Old-
        Fashioned, 39
Cinnamon Wonder Waffles, 22
Cline, Elmer, 1–2
Cobbler, Wonder Pear, 66
Continental Baking Company, 4
Cornflakes
    Wonder Omelet Sandwiches, 49
Crab, Mrs. Proctor's Devilled, 94
Creamed Fish in Wonder Patty Shells, 93
Cream of celery soup
    Wonderfully Crunchy Chicken
        Casserole, 59
Cream of mushroom soup
    A Perfectly Wonderful Casserole, 57
    Wonder Beef Cups, 41

    Wonderfully Crunchy Chicken
        Casserole, 59
Crêpes Suzette, Wonderful, 79–80
Crullers, Wonder, 25

● ● **D** ● ●

Delicious Lenten Pudding, 95
De Luxe Bridge Loaf, 89
Desserts
    All-American Peach Pie Wonder, 67
    Delicious Lenten Pudding, 95
    Grandma's Wonder Bread Pudding
        with Lemon Sauce, 83
    The Most Wonderful Apple Pie
        Squares, 64
    Top-of-the-Morning Wonder Bread
        Pudding, 78
    Wonder Apricot Pudding, 85
    Wonder Blintzes, 28
    Wonder Caramel Apple Bread
        Pudding, 82
    Wonder Cream Cheese Bites, 30
    Wonder Easter Egg Sandwich, 74
    Wonderful Crêpes Suzette, 79–80
    Wonderful Napoleon, 71–72
    Wonder Pear Cobbler, 66
    Wonderstrudel, 69–70
Doughnuts
    Wonder Crullers, 25

● ● **E** ● ●

Easter Egg Sandwich, Wonder, 74
Eggs
    Baked Wonder Omelet, 18
    De Luxe Bridge Loaf, 89
    Jellied Eggs, 92

Eggs, *continued*
    Wonder Bread Eggs, 14
    Wonder Eggs Royale, 23
    Wonderful Bird's Nest, 15
    Wonder Omelet Sandwiches, 49

● ● **F, G** ● ●

Fish, Creamed, in Wonder Patty Shells, 93
Grandma's Wonder Bread Pudding with
    Lemon Sauce, 83
Grilled Baloney and Wonder, 47
Grilled Peanut Butter, Jelly, and Wonder,
    44

● ● **H** ● ●

Ham
    De Luxe Bridge Loaf, 89
    Wonder Omelet Sandwiches, 49
Happy Wonder Bakers, 4

● ● **I, J** ● ●

Interstate Bakeries Corporation, 10
Jellied Eggs, 92
Jelly
    Delicious Lenten Pudding, 95
    Grilled Peanut Butter, Jelly, and
      Wonder, 44

● ● **L** ● ●

Lamb
    Pilgrim Pies, 88
Lemon Sauce, 83

● ● **M** ● ●

Marshmallows
    Delicious Lenten Pudding, 95
    The Most Wonderful Apple Pie
      Squares, 64
Mrs. Proctor's Devilled Crab, 94
Mushrooms
    Wonderfully Crunchy Chicken
      Casserole, 59
    Wonder Sausage and Peppers, 50

● ● **N** ● ●

Napoleon, Wonderful, 71–72
New York World's Fair, 6

● ● **O** ● ●

Old-Fashioned Cinnamon Wonder Toast,
    39
Omelets
    Baked Wonder Omelet, 18
    Wonder Omelet Sandwiches, 49
Oranges
    Wonderful Crêpes Suzette, 79–80

● ● **P** ● ●

Peach Pie Wonder, All-American, 67
Peanut butter
    Grilled Peanut Butter, Jelly, and
      Wonder, 44
    Wonder Trail Mix Sandwich, 51
Pears
    Tropical Wonder Casserole, 60
    Wonder Pear Cobbler, 66
Peppers
    Wonder Bread Pepper Snack, 34
    Wonder Sausage and Peppers, 50

A Perfectly Wonderful Casserole, 57
Pigs in a Wonder Blanket, 17
Pilgrim Pies, 88
Pineapple
    Tropical Wonder Casserole, 60
Pork. *See also* Bacon; Ham; Sausage
    Swedish Pork Chops, 90
Potato chips
    Wonder Chip "Wich," 46
    Wonder Omelet Sandwiches, 49
Potatoes
    Pilgrim Pies, 88
Proctor, Alice Adams, 5, 6
Pudding
    Delicious Lenten Pudding, 95
    Grandma's Wonder Bread Pudding
        with Lemon Sauce, 83
    Top-of-the-Morning Wonder Bread
        Pudding, 78
    Wonder Apricot Pudding, 85
    Wonder Caramel Apple Bread
        Pudding, 82
    Wonderful Napoleon, 71–72

● ● **R** ● ●

Raisins
    Grandma's Wonder Bread Pudding
        with Lemon Sauce, 83
    The Most Wonderful Apple Pie
        Squares, 64
    Top-of-the-Morning Wonder Bread
        Pudding, 78
    Wonder Trail Mix Sandwich, 51

● ● **S** ● ●

Sandwiches
    Grilled Baloney and Wonder, 47
    Grilled Peanut Butter, Jelly, and
        Wonder, 44
    Wonder Chip "Wich," 46
    Wonder Easter Egg Sandwich, 74
    Wonder Eggs Royale, 23
    Wonder Kid Sandwiches, 52
    Wonder Omelet Sandwiches, 49
    Wonder Sausage and Peppers, 50
    Wonder Trail Mix Sandwich, 51
Sausage
    Apple Wonder Waffles, 19–20
    Baked Wonder Omelet, 18
    Pigs in a Wonder Blanket, 17
    Wonder Sausage and Peppers, 50
Strawberries
    Wonderful Napoleon, 71–72
Strudel, Wonder-, 69–70
Swedish Pork Chops, 90
Sweetened Tomato and Wonder
    Casserole, 58

● ● **T** ● ●

Taggart Baking Company, 1–4
Three Wonderful Pieces, 31
Toast, Old-Fashioned Cinnamon
    Wonder, 39
Tomato and Wonder Casserole,
    Sweetened, 58
Top-of-the-Morning Wonder Bread
    Pudding, 78
Tropical Wonder Casserole, 60

W

Waffles
    Apple Wonder Waffles, 19–20
    Cinnamon Wonder Waffles, 22
Walnuts
    The Most Wonderful Apple Pie
        Squares, 64
Water chestnuts
    Wonderfully Crunchy Chicken
        Casserole, 59
Wonder Apricot Pudding, 85
Wonder Asparagus Rolls to Die For, 36–38
Wonder Beef Cups, 41
Wonder Blintzes, 28
Wonder Bread. *See also* individual recipes
    advertising campaigns for, 4–10
    cellophane-wrapped, 9
    introduction of, 1–4
    nutrition and, 7–8
    popularity of, 1, 10–11
    round, 9
    sliced, 5

Wonder Bread Balls, 35
Wonder Bread Eggs, 14
Wonder Bread Pepper Snack, 34
Wonder Caramel Apple Bread Pudding,
    82
Wonder Chip "Wich," 46
Wonder Cream Cheese Bites, 30
Wonder Crullers, 25
Wonder Easter Egg Sandwich, 74
Wonder Eggs Royale, 23
Wonderful Bird's Nest, 15
Wonderful Crêpes Suzette, 79–80
Wonderfully Crunchy Chicken Casserole,
    59
Wonderful Napoleon, 71–72
Wonder Kid Sandwiches, 52
Wonder Omelet Sandwiches, 49
Wonder Parmesan Bread, 33
Wonder Pear Cobbler, 66
Wonder Sausage and Peppers, 50
Wonderstrudel, 69–70
Wonder Trail Mix Sandwich, 51